AF375489

# Family

Like branches on a tree, we all grow in different directions.
Yet our roots remain as one.

This is a work of nonfiction, written by my grandfather, David LaWayne Hanks, before his passing. He spent a great deal of time on the Teton Mountain Range herding sheep with his brothers. As he shared this experience with me, it was clear that it was a life-changing moment in which God became real to him. This account is taken from his personal writings. Slight changes have been made from the original works to better fit a children's book format.  Front Cover artwork painted by WylaGene Seal, niece of David & Elen Hanks. The original painting currently hangs in Mary Bennett's home. Artwork inside the book was painted by David's granddaughter Silvia D. J. Romleski.



First edition

Book design by Mary J Bennett

ISBN 979-8-8690-5700-6

# The Lost Sheep

## A Young Boy's Answered Prayer

Written by: David LaWayne Hanks

Compiled by: Mary J Bennett

Illustrated by: Silvia D J Romleski

Cover Art by: WylaGene Seal

"Consequently, even though our summertime experiences were lonely and difficult, I am aware that the environment of the mountains can become sacred on occasions. During a summer, five or six years after this experience, I carried a *Book of Mormon* with me while herding sheep. Carrying it in my saddlebags, I would take it out as occasion permitted and quietly read in the shade of a pine or aspen tree. I felt the spirit of that great book as I read it for the first time and pondered its meaning under the quiet influence of the mountains."

-David LaWayne Hanks

*David LaWayne Hanks - Teton Mountains*

I have felt a certain affinity with Moses, Nephi, or the Brother of

Jared as they went into the mountains.  It was there that I also

was favored with a great spiritual experience.

*Wright & David picking berries*

One day during late summer while the sheep were grazing in the

southwest corner of the coal lands, up under the rim beyond

which lay Sheep Basin, we lost some sheep. My older brother,

Wright, left me to watch the herd while he scouted around

looking for signs that might lead us to those that were lost.

*David LaWayne Hanks*

During that long day, I tried to keep track of the sheep. In that area were many ridges and ravines and above those, an extremely steep and brushy hillside. Some spots were almost impassible.

*David Hanks - Driggs Family Farm*

In the late afternoon, I put salt out for the sheep and working

around the edge of the herd, began pushing them slowly toward

the bedground.

One becomes accustomed to the size of the herd and even though the number approximated 3,100, it is possible to note even a slight change in the size. It was obvious as the herd gathered together that evening that a sizeable number were missing.

*David LaWayne Hanks*

Immediately, I became alarmed. I had let Wright down. He had

trusted me with the sheep. I had betrayed my family's trust.

Here was our livelihood. We were carrying a sacred trust and I

had been careless and failed to honor that trust.

*David LaWayne Hanks hearding sheep*

I rode some distance from the herd, where the noise of the congregating sheep could not be heard and listened carefully in every direction. Riding a little farther, I listened again. Nothing. I was hoping to hear the bleat of ewes searching for their lambs or the sound of sheep bells. Sound travels a great distance in the quiet of evening, but I could hear nothing. What could I do?

*Emma Wright Hulet Hanks*

I had been taught to pray at Mother's knee when I was very young and on many occasions afterward, though not regularly, I had turned to Him in prayer. Consequently, my first response in this desperate situation was to turn to my Heavenly Father for assistance.

*David LaWayne Hanks with his pack horses*

There in the stillness of the mountains… in the sacred solitude of those stately pines, I dismounted and knelt by the side of my horse. I pleaded with my Father in Heaven for help.  I prayed, first asking forgiveness for my negligence, and then asking for help to find the sheep. My horse stood silently beside me. The reins were held in my hand.

*David LaWayne Hanks - Driggs*

During those sacred moments while still pleading, I heard the sound of a bell loudly and clearly in the evening air. Recognizing this as a direct answer to my desperate prayer and expressing my appreciation to my Heavenly Father, I arose from my knees a much stronger and more confident boy.

Heading in the direction from which the sound of the bell had

come, I rode and rode. Finally, after a distance seeming far

beyond the range of sound over ridges and through ravines, I

found the sheep. It seemed impossible that sound could have

traveled that far. Yet I had heard that sheep bell ring loudly and

clearly. I knew that my prayer had been heard and answered.

Carefully rounding up the sheep, I moved them quickly toward

the bedground where we arrived after dark.

<br>
*David LaWayne Hanks - Sheepcamp*

For years, I blamed myself for negligence and carelessness during that day. However, as I think about that experience from the perspective of many years, I am much less inclined to feel guilty. I was only 12 years old and certainly not very wise to the demands of constant attention required while herding sheep.

I believe that my Father in Heaven recognized this also as he heard and answered my prayer. In addition, I realize now that few boys my age were really capable of meeting the trials that we encountered daily on the summer range.

*David LaWayne Hanks*

This experience has become one of the most meaningful and spiritual of my entire life. I knew, as I know to this day, that my prayer had been answered. This testimony has been a great strength to me and has given me the faith to pray on many subsequent occasions expecting an answer, just as I received on that sacred occasion.

# Song of the Saddle

By: David LaWayne Hanks
From his book: "Musings of an Ex-Sheepherder"

Lonely on the mountain,
Thoughts are drifting far,
And childhood dreams are soaring past
The Twinkling evening star.
Sing, Sing, you saddle,
Sing his cares away;
Lift his heart and hold it close
For yet another day.

Riding up the timbered slopes
Toward the azure sky;
If he were in a rocket ship,
To distant parts he'd fly.
Sing, Sing, You Saddle,
Sing his cares away;
There on that far off planet,
He'd find an easier way.

Riding through an aspen grove,
It's beauty soft and keen;
The warbler and the meadow lark
A special carol sing.
Sing, Sing, You Saddle,
Sing his cares away;
In cadence with the lovely song,
Please let this moment stay.

Ever on we travel,
Day after quiet day,
Riding herd on boyhood dreams
Lest they break away.
Sing, Sing, you saddle,
Sing his cares away;
And Cherish each small moment
Where childhood hopes are laid

Sitting by the campfire,
Flames are dancing high,
Just to send a message,
An Answer to his sigh
Sing, sing, you saddle,
Sing his cares away;
Guard him through the darkened night
Into another day.

Quiet on the mountain,
Yearning boyhood heart
Fun and friends are miles away,
Lonely, lonely heart.
Sing, Sing, You Saddle,
Sing his cares away;
Bring into his heaving soul
A lighter, brighter ray.

Clippety, cloppety ever,
Is there not a thrill
When horse and singing saddle
Climb each unnamed hill?
Sing, Sing, you saddle,
Sing his cares away;
That horse and boy together
Could climb the Milky Way.

Gazing at the drifting clouds,
With ever changing forms,
To watch the panoroma
Where boyhood hopes are borne.
Sing, sing, you saddle,
Sing his cares away;
Lay me on a fleecy cloud
And let me dream away.

# DAVID LAWAYNE HANKS

David LaWayne Hanks was born October 5, 1925 to David Capener Hanks and Emma Wright Hulet in Tetonia, Teton, Idaho. He was the 6th of 9 children. When David was just 7 years old, his father unexpectedly died of pneumonia, leaving the family to manage the sheep farm in Driggs, Idaho.

David and his brothers spent every summer leading their herd of sheep to graze through the Teton mountain range. Those were long, hot, dusty days but proved to be the learning grounds for the making of men. Men strong in faith and strong in character. David often spoke of those years with mixed emotions. He spoke of the weariness he found in the strenuous and monotonous work, but also of gratitude. Gratitude for the love of God he found in the stillness of the mountains.

He married Elen Wallace on June 15, 1949 in Idaho Falls, Idaho and together they raised 7 children. They lived in many parts of the country as David pursued his doctorate degree and subsequently worked in the field of microbiology. They were both known for their open hospitality and dedication to sharing with others their love of Jesus Christ. They welcomed hundreds into their home and offered kindness to all those they knew. David passed away on September 2, 2017 In Logan, Utah and was buried under the shade of a stately pine in the Cache Valley Cemetery.

*Emma Hanks Family - back: Adrian*
*middle: Lincoln, Wright, Davida, Clair*
*front: Phillip (insert), Betty, Louise, David*

*David & Elen - quilting- Albuquerque, NM*

*Elen & David - farewell from branch in Missouri*

*David Hanks - 1970's - professor at*
*Northwest Missouri State University, St. Louis Missouri*

*4 generations - abt 1951*
*David, Great Grandma Alice (Betsy) Hulet,*
*Grandma Emma Hanks, Lecia, Dave*

*David Hanks - missionary - abt 1944*

Elen, David, Lecia - abt 1951

Elen, David, Lecia - Driggs, ID

Clair, David, Wright, Lincoln - US Navy WWII

David & Elen, Lecia, Dave, Steve, Aaron (by age) - 1957

Davida, Wright, Lincoln, Clair, David, Eileen (Earl's daughter), Betty
Listed by age

David & Elen Hanks wedding day - June 15, 1949
Idaho Falls, ID

# David LaWayne Hanks - Family Tree

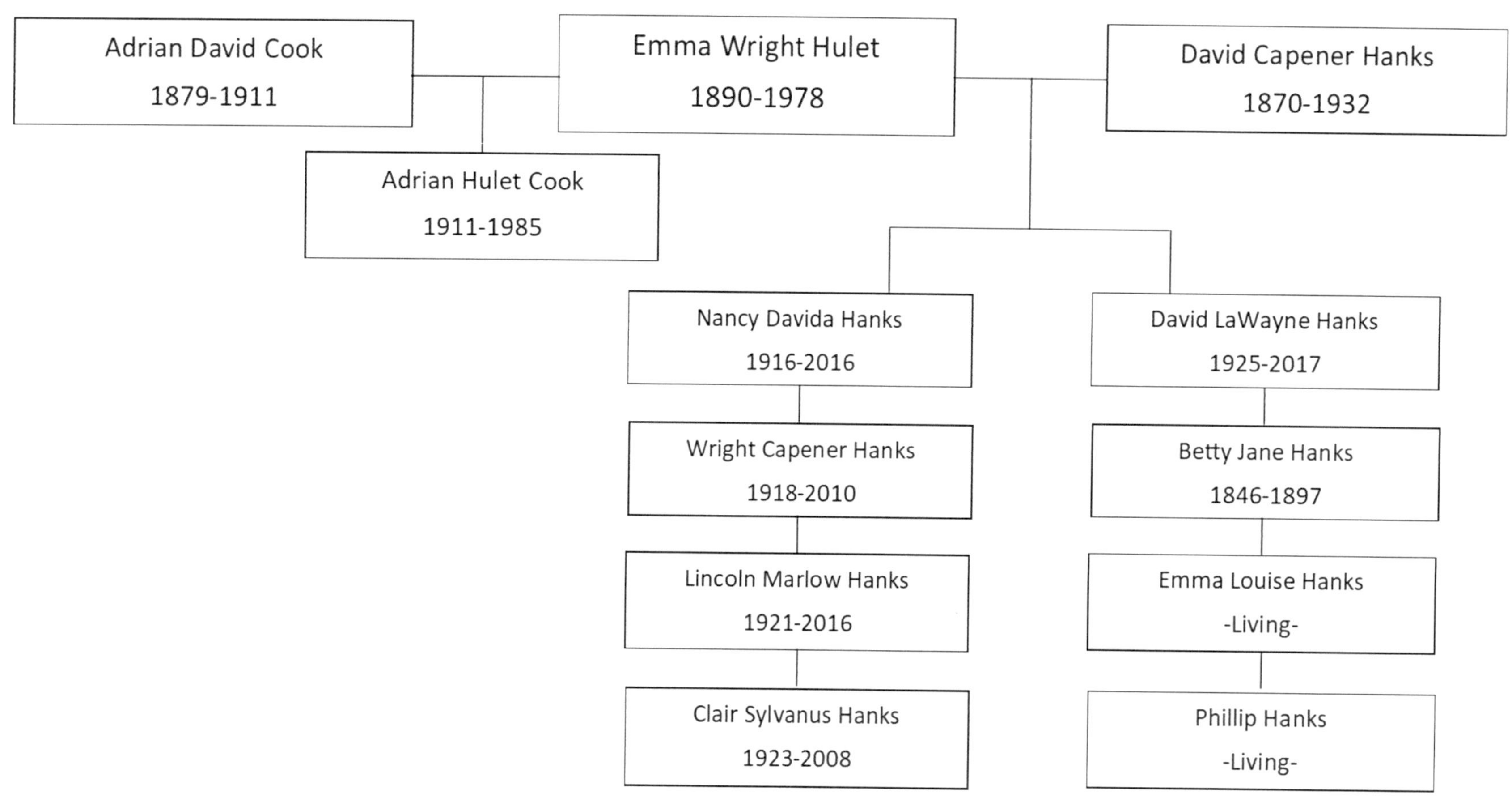